Hippos Sort Socks

by Amar Ganeesh
illustrated by John Berg

HOUGHTON MIFFLIN   BOSTON

Copyright © by Houghton Mifflin Company. All rights reserved.

No part of this work may be reproduced or transmitted in any form or by any means, electronic or mechanical, including photocopying or recording, or by any information storage or retrieval system without the prior written permission of Houghton Mifflin Company unless such copying is expressly permitted by federal copyright law. Address inquiries to School Permissions, Houghton Mifflin Company, 222 Berkeley Street, Boston, MA 02116.

Printed in China

ISBN 10: 0-618-88628-1
ISBN 13: 978-0-618-88628-9

7 8 9 10 0940 16 15 14
4500466952

Hippo and Fox washed socks.
They put them up to dry.

2   How many socks did they wash?

Hippo's socks are big.
Fox's socks are small.

How are their socks different?

3

Hippo gets 2 socks with dots.
Fox gets 2 socks with no dots.

How are these socks the same?

Hippo looks at the socks.
He gives 1 to Fox.

How are these socks different? 5

They get the last 2 socks.
Now, they have all their socks.

6   How are Hippo's socks all the same?

Off they go to play.
Hooray! Hooray!

How are the socks the same now? 7

Responding

Math Concepts

Sock Sort

Draw
1. Draw 2 big socks.
2. Draw 2 small socks.

Tell About Compare and Contrast
1. Tell who had big socks.
2. Tell who had small socks.

Write
Write the words *big* and *small*.